Back the Brink

Contents

Introduction	2
1 Sea otters	4
2 Humpback whales	10
3 Bengal tigers	16
4 Peregrine falcons	22
Glossary	28
Index	29
Back from the brink	30

Written by Inbali Iserles

Collins

Introduction

Humans are changing the planet in lots of ways. We have built cities to live in and farms to grow the food we eat. Sometimes human activity has caused problems for other animals, and this has led to the disappearance of those animals from our land, seas and air. But people are helping nature to fight back against **extinction**.

In recent years, some amazing animals have been saved from the brink of extinction by the passion and effort of their human protectors. Let's celebrate those animals, and the people who work to keep them safe.

wildlife vet: treats sick and injured animals

campaigner: makes people take notice of problems

park ranger: protects wildlife areas

1 Sea otters

Animal: sea otter
Eats: fish, shellfish, crabs and sea urchins
Habitat: mostly at sea but some come onto land to rest
Location: Pacific Ocean in North America and Asia
Population: about 130,000 worldwide

Sea otters are **mammals** that spend most of their lives at sea. They even give birth on the water! The young otters rest and drink milk while floating on their mothers' tummies.

● **location of sea otters**

Sea otters may look cute but they're **apex predators**. They love to eat the sea urchins that feed on underwater kelp forests. By munching their way through plenty of urchins, the otters stop the kelp from being **overrun** and destroyed. This helps to protect the health and **biodiversity** of oceans.

The otters rest in the kelp, hooking onto its thick stems so they don't drift away.

Fact box

Sea otters are social. They often "hold hands" when they sleep so they stay with their friends.

Saving sea otters

Sea otters have thick coats that keep them dry in the water. Sadly, this led to humans hunting them almost to extinction. The otters' coats were used to make clothes for humans. In 1911, there were fewer than 2,000 sea otters worldwide.

The fur trade used to be big business.

America passed laws to protect sea otters, but the **species** was still in trouble. Fishing, mining and drilling were damaging the kelp forests and harming the otters.

Thanks to the hard work of **conservation** groups, marine-protected areas that ban these harmful activities were set up along American coastlines where sea otters live. Otter numbers have grown in these areas. We need more protected spaces where wildlife can thrive!

2 Humpback whales

Animal: humpback whale
Eats: krill and fish like anchovies and sardines
Habitat: oceans and seas
Location: a worldwide range
Population: 60,000 worldwide

Humpback whales are huge marine mammals that are found in every ocean of the world. They are **filter feeders**, drawing in huge numbers of krill and fish. Adults are about 15 metres long – that's the length of a bus!

● location of humpback whales

Fact box

Humpback whales often "talk" or "sing" to each other. Humpback songs are a mysterious combination of moans, clicks and cries that travel for many kilometres under the ocean. Whales in the same part of the ocean are known to repeat the same song.

Threats to whales

For thousands of years, humans hunted whales for their oil and meat. Tragically, around 100 years ago, there were only a few thousand humpback whales left throughout the oceans of the world. Other whales like sperm whales and fin whales were also in trouble.

whale hunters in 1920

a fin whale

Saving humpback whales

In the 1970s, a conservation group called Greenpeace set out to **confront** a hunting ship. The group tried to stop the hunt by putting their boat between the whales and the ship. They played humpback whale songs on loudspeakers.

Greenpeace members use a boat to disrupt whale hunting.

a group of protesters outside the UK Parliament

This was the beginning of a battle to show ordinary people that whales should be protected. "Save the Whales" became the **slogan** of the worldwide wildlife conservation movement.

Most whale hunting was banned in the 1980s. The results have been amazing. Humpback whale populations are almost back to pre-hunting numbers.

There are still threats to whales like pollution, over-fishing and climate change. Let's keep fighting for whales so their songs continue to echo through the oceans for generations to come.

3 Bengal tigers

Animal: Bengal tiger (India)
Eats: deer and other animals like wild boar, birds, fish and lizards
Habitat: forests, swamps or grasslands
Location: found in 20 states of India
Population: about 3,700 tigers in India

Tigers are the world's biggest cats. The largest type – the Amur tiger – is as long as a small car and as heavy as five adult humans. Different types of tiger are found across Asia. They are all apex predators and excellent hunters.

India

● location of tiger reserves in India

Fact box

Tigers have famously loud roars. They can be heard from as far as three kilometres away!

Don't stand too close! Tigers are usually **solitary**.

Tigers in trouble

Tigers once roamed across Asia but their numbers have plummeted in recent years. **Human development** means that tigers don't have enough wild places to live. Farmers sometimes kill tigers that prey on their sheep or goats. People hunt them for their beautiful coats, their bones and even their meat. Sadly, some types of tiger are already extinct and, in other parts of South Asia, the Bengal tiger is still in trouble. But India is proving that it is possible to protect this vulnerable animal.

tourists taking photos of a wild Bengal tiger in Ranthambore National Park, Rajasthan, India

Saving India's tigers

Conservation organisations like the Born Free Foundation are working with people in India to protect **nature reserves** where tigers live. They monitor the tigers, try to stop human development close to reserves and help local farmers find safer locations.

Tigers have almost doubled in India from fewer than 2,000 in the 1970s to about 3,700. Although these are still small numbers, it proves that hard work and dedication can save this incredible cat.

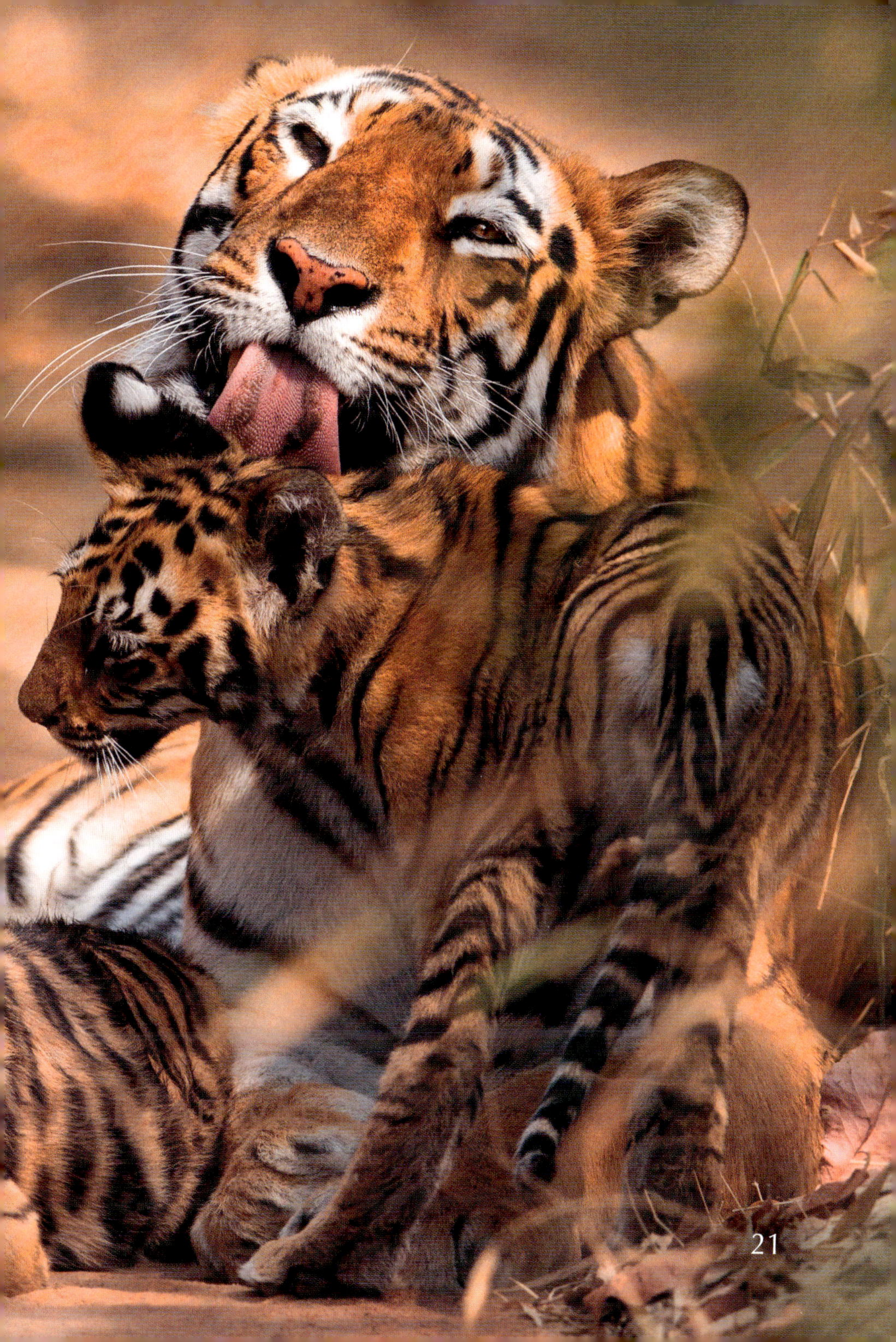

4 Peregrine falcons

Animal: peregrine falcon
Eats: smaller birds
Habitat: open countryside, coastal regions and cities
Location: every continent except Antarctica
Population: 250,000 to 500,000 worldwide

Peregrine falcons are famous for their speed. These birds of prey can dive-bomb smaller birds at up to 320 kilometres per hour. That's three times faster than most trains! Peregrine falcons usually live in the countryside and coastal areas. But because they aren't fussy eaters, they have **adapted** to city life too. They can be found roosting on bridges and high-rise buildings.

Fact box
Watch out, pigeons! The peregrine falcon is the fastest animal on Earth.

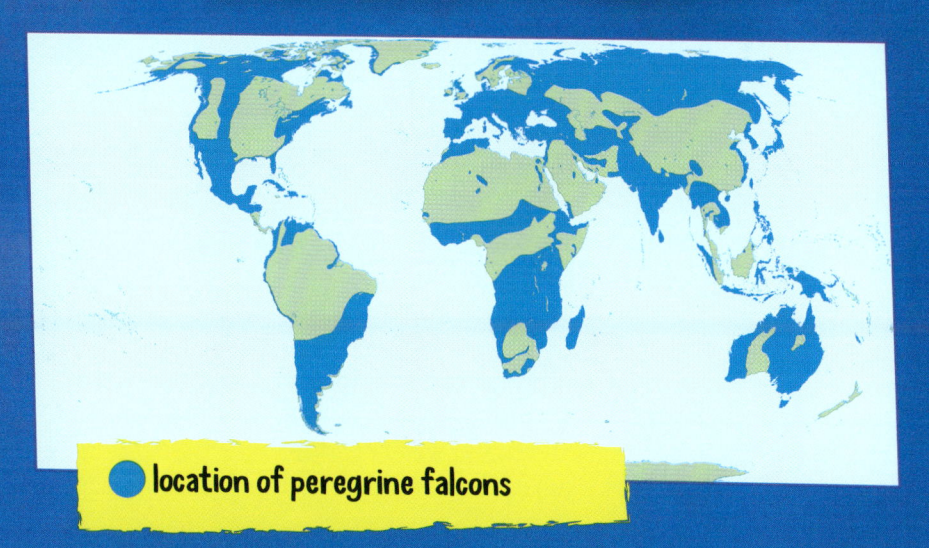

● location of peregrine falcons

Like sea otters and tigers, peregrine falcons are apex predators. They live on all continents except Antarctica. Some peregrine falcons migrate – often for many thousands of miles – while others stay put.

Fact box

Birds like Canada geese fly to warmer climates when the weather gets cold. Other birds, like mallard ducks, do not usually migrate: they tend to stay in the same location all year.

Canada geese

mallard ducks

Saving the peregrine falcon

Over the last hundred years, peregrine falcons started to disappear. Scientists figured out that "DDT", a powerful **pesticide** used in farming to kill insects, was the biggest threat to the falcons.

DDT weakened the falcons' eggs, with few chicks surviving to adulthood. The population was heading towards global extinction.

Farms are sprayed with DDT.

Insects are covered in DDT.

26

DDT was found to be very harmful to the environment, including humans. It was banned across large parts of the world in the 1970s. Scientists also started to breed peregrine falcons and release them into the wild. Thanks to their efforts, peregrine falcon numbers have soared in one of the greatest extinction reversal stories of our time.

Those insects are eaten by small birds.

The birds are eaten by peregrine falcons.

All over the world, people are working together to save endangered animals. Alongside laws banning hunting, wildlife protection areas have led to growing numbers of sea otters on American coastlines, and tigers in India. Humpback whales are thriving in our oceans since most whaling stopped, and a ban on pesticides has seen peregrine falcons glide over Earth's skies.

Together we can protect the diversity of our planet. Let's all become voices for wildlife, big and small, and cheer for the animals brought back from the brink.

Glossary

adapted changed over time to fit in with an environment
apex predator a meat-eating animal that does not have any natural enemies
biodiversity the number and variety of different animals, plants and fungi found in a place
confront to stand up boldly to someone
conservation the protection of wildlife
extinction when a type of animal, plant or fungus dies out
filter feeders sea animals that feed by sifting the water for tiny creatures like krill

human development things like houses, shops, farms and factories

mammals warm-blooded animals that give birth to live babies and feed them on milk

nature reserves areas of land where nature is protected

overrun to have too much

pesticide something used to kill insects, usually on farms

slogan a few words used to advertise a political idea or sell things

solitary on your own

species a group of animals, plants or fungi

Index

conservation/ists 9, 14–15, 20

food 2, 4, 6, 10–11, 16, 22

habitat 4, 10, 16, 22

humans 2–3, 8, 13, 17, 19, 20, 27

hunting 8, 13–15, 19, 28

mammals 5, 11

migration 24

predators 6, 17, 24

Back from the brink

Animal: sea otter
Extinction threat: hunting and habitat loss
Saved by: hunting ban and wildlife protection areas

Animal: humpback whale
Extinction threat: hunting
Saved by: a ban on most hunting

30

Animal: Bengal tiger, India
Extinction threat: illegal hunting and habitat loss
Saved by: local support and monitoring

Animal: peregrine falcon
Extinction threat: DDT pesticide
Saved by: a ban on DDT in most countries

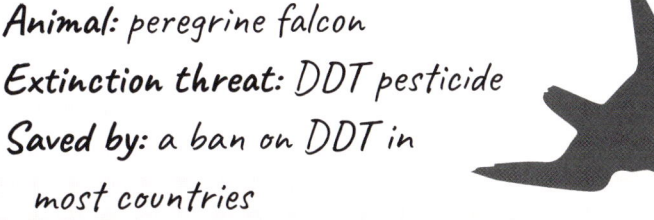

Ideas for reading

Written by Gill Matthews
Primary Literacy Consultant

Reading objectives:
- check that the text makes sense to them, discuss their understanding and explaining the meaning of words in context
- identify main ideas drawn from more than one paragraph and summarising these
- retrieve and record information from non-fiction

Spoken language objectives:
- use relevant strategies to build their vocabulary
- use spoken language to develop understanding through speculating, hypothesising, imagining and exploring ideas
- participate in discussions, presentations, performances, role play, improvisations and debates

Curriculum links: Science: animals, including humans

Interest words: habitat, location, population

Build a context for reading

- Show children the front cover. Ask what animal they can see.
- Read the title. Ask children what it means to them. Check their understanding of the word *brink*.
- Read the back-cover blurb. Ask children what they expect to find out from the book.
- Point out that this is an information book. Ask children what features they expect to find in the book.
- Ask children to find the contents page. Discuss the purpose and organisation of a contents page.

Understand and apply reading strategies

- Ask children to find the chapter called Introduction. Read pp2–3 aloud.
- Challenge children to summarise the information given on these pages. Explore whether it has changed their ideas of what they expect to find out from the book.